Mystery Schools

Bruce MacKinnon

For Maryann —
Best Wishes —

Bon Mac

Washington Writers' Publishing House
Washington, DC

Library of Congress Cataloging-in-Publication Data
MacKinnon, Bruce, 1950-
    Mystery schools / Bruce MacKinnon.
        p.   cm.
    ISBN-10: 0-931846-88-9
    ISBN-13: 978-0-931846-88-5
    I. Title.
    PS3613.M2727M97   2007
    811'.6—dc22   2007025150

Book design and composition: Sarah Ely
Cover design: Sarah Ely
Cover art: Jessie MacKinnon
Author photo: Jessie MacKinnon
Printed in the United States of America by McNaughton & Gunn, Inc.

Acknowledgments and publishing history may be found on page 69.

Publication of this book was made possible by the friends and members of the
Washington Writers' Publishing House
P.O. Box 15271
Washington, DC 20003
www.wwph.org

For Jessie—
in this and all possible lifetimes

Contents

Behind the Walls

Without

Fate, you might call it, the gods
choreographing the morning events.
Late for the bus, crossing the street
to catch the next. This is tragedy,
everyone seems to agree, the suddenness,

the violence, the irony, the age
of the man, not much older than me.
Although we hardly knew each other,
something like shock waves batter my house
half way down the block from his.

Love at first sight, the minister says,
met her in a flower shop. I think
of my son and how he will withdraw
his love from his mother and me,
if he's lucky, finding someone suddenly,

without warning in some flower shop.
People stand and tell stories.
The church is packed. *He drove across
town for orange pineapple ice cream
one year for my birthday.* Chaos,

she says, with a sweep of her hand,
is out there. Like a great beast,
we turn to look through the windows
where the evening begins,
the sky a broken blue in the trees,

the sun, a stain on the horizon,
just beyond the amphitheater,
where we gather beneath the cross,
heavy as a man, that hangs in the center,
suspended by wires you can hardly see.

Kozlow

I saw him at the gas pump the other day.
I had to look two or three times—same wire brush hair,
same graying beard, basset hound eyes. Sometimes
a person will go underground. Sometimes you only
dream a death. But he merely pumped gas, looked
past me. If he were a spirit, he would have done
more, the man who sat down at the piano
and played when the x-rays came back filled with holes.
He would, at least, have smiled, as if to say
forget it, rolled his eyes and shrugged his shoulders.
That's what I would do if I were the one to come back,
inhabiting, say, a tree, as my son walked by,
heavy with himself, trapped by his body. I'd bend
when there was no wind, rustle my branches
for him, drop a leaf in his ear.

Mud Angel

Love affairs come in all sizes and shapes
and I can't remember all of the ones I've had.
Sometimes I try to count them, but it's no use,
and I do it only half-heartedly, embarrassing
myself as I try to remember, wondering why this
could possibly be important. To find a fixed
number, I suppose, is the answer, in a random,
impossible universe. There are starting points,
origins, at least in myth, at least in conscious
memory, and if we're pinning *love* and *affair*
together to mean *sex,* to mean initiation, then
it would begin in a darkened bedroom in the middle
of one afternoon, done quickly and without much
pleasure, except, I suppose, the pleasure of guilt
and pride in accomplishment. But not the kind
felt earlier, down in Kim Glad's basement, my
guitar playing buddy, Ronnie Bond and I taking
turns, Kim letting us take turns kissing her,
where she would rank me second out of two, but
that was okay. And though her hair was cut close
and tight, and she kept all buttons buttoned,
I remember how warm and wet her mouth was, how
she wore the kind of lipstick, maybe it was called
Slicker, that was pale and fashionable, that let
you slide down her face, mouth to cheek to chin
to fall off her face and into the unknown, the way
sometimes when you're out walking in the rain
you'll get so drenched it makes no difference if
you lie down suddenly and begin to swim, or wave
your arms and legs back and forth like the universal
man, to put wings and a halo on your mud angel.

Stories

He's gone, like a right arm, like the sky lowered
to half-mast, but she's here, telling me of the years
she doesn't remember, after her parents lost the house,
after the nickels my grandfather saved by walking were
finally not enough. Even this much I haven't heard
before, or forgotten, and I'm salting away everything
she says these days, every slip, every crack that leaves
the usually hidden exposed. Watching carefully,
the way you'd read a label, suddenly aware of the harm
a few milligrams can cause, I catch a glimpse
of the scar that runs up her chest, that peeks out
at the top of her nightgown, where the dark and silver
hair falls as I brush it down. And the sore, strong
freckled back that I massage with liniment, loosening
the knots of inflammation, small side effects
of the new arteries that grow up her heart
like vines up a trellis.

The Butter Knife

I'm holding the butter knife in my hand
that my son gave me when he was half my size,
that he worked on all year long, whittling and
whittling until it fits now, comfortably in my palm.
It's made of ash and is not a thing of beauty.
There are only a few people in the world
who would look at it and cherish it, decide
that it should be put away with the other keepsakes
in whatever box that would be the first thing grabbed
in case of fire. I found it in the St. Anthony drawer,
where lost things are sometimes found again. Time
will not come back, and I don't want it to. Time
is the great fire, needing most of what we do
to keep burning, needing to feed on what we think
and how we love. The butter knife will go
in my green file cabinet that—if you should be the one
called upon, if there's a fire—you'll find on the floor
of my closet—just a small file with a surfer's cross,
some brown love beads, a safety patrol pin, some letters,
and a few more, essentially worthless knickknacks.
The butter knife has buttered toast and spread jam.
It had a companion, the pumpkin knife, that had teeth
so dull, not even a child could cut himself with it.
It was mostly used to make vegetable soup, usually on
winter days when time burned slow, when there was no
school except that taught by father to son and son
to father. I think the pumpkin knife is older, and is gone,
and if it turns up, if it comes back—like Eurydice
from the underworld—it will still not be saved.

Connections

I've looked in this pocket and that, searched
for it as it traveled like Bloom's throwaway,
the one that found its way from pocket to pocket,
then finally into the Liffy, only to float, like
the little wooden Indian in *Paddle to the Sea,*

the book my mother read to me one rainy
afternoon, all day in and out on the periphery of
consciousness. It's like that, almost on the tip
of the tongue, almost, just beyond the taste buds,
just nestled at the back of the throat, beyond

the tonsils, if they were still there, cut away
long ago, gone in an ether dream, a whirlpool
of vanishing sense. It's like that, the sudden
loss, then the blood, this idea that I had,
that I don't remember, that I thought was safely

tucked away, like in a hope chest, a trousseau,
an outfit, an old Nehru jacket that I'd thought saved,
only to discover it—or not to, and that's the point,
gone, vanished—gone again. And it was somehow
connected, I think, to the shooting this morning

or the one, years ago, my friend and his wife . . . .
But what was the connection, did it unweave itself
by night, did it refuse to yield to one hiding under
a seal skin, who took ten years to travel home, and still
not get there, or if he did, find everything changed,

the long bow rusted, the arrows rotten, the lover gone?

From the Mesozoic

And so it comes to rest in our house,
in my son's possession, dark and heavy,
volcano gray, transformed one day, one year,
some time before flood and ice, each cell

gathering weight, crystallizing into
this piece I'm holding, marked with knotholes
and tooth marks of some insect,
some sibling on the evolutionary line

whose art and craft brought down this tree,
sinking it deep in mud and ash, silica
shining from its pores, mummy, relic,
shell, plaster cast. A million years later

the Beatles play from my son's boom box;
his duck-blond head bobs to the music
we both love—John Lennon in the studio,
chewing gum, headphones on, surrounded

by the orchestra in tuxedos, singing
All you need is love. Through the window,
clouds are all resembling cities, creatures
from the Mesozoic, friends who drift,

getting thinner and thinner. Don't talk
about me when I'm gone, burn the tapes
that line the shelves, let the mystery stay.
When he turns off the music, he asks

what happens when you sleep, where do you go.
Bedtime comes too soon, when I'll pull
the covers up over his head, then down again
as he sleeps under the fan's slow circles.

Behind the Walls

After they gutted the ceiling of our kitchen,
I asked the plumbers if they'd found any hidden treasure.
No, they assured me, not even a rat's shrunken carcass.

This is like God—a spinning coin that falls sometimes to one side,
sometimes to the other. This is because I am not filled with grace,
which can't be earned—you can't get there from here because

you already are. Therefore, there's treasure behind the walls:
my grandfather, the carpenter, hid some here in this house
that was once theirs. I can feel it in my hollow bones, swear to it

by the dust he's turned to, by the unsteady earth beneath the unsteady
floor of our house. I'm sure I saw it in his eyes, as they carried him
down the stairs on a stretcher, as I patted his hair and the ambulance

took us to the doors, where we parted, and he lay in white sheets
in a white room. When I look into the mirror, I can see it
wavering, like a candle flame, in the eye's deep cave.

In a Cabin in the Woods

Here I am, sitting in a cabin in the woods
thinking about my lost lives.
If I were a drunk I'd be drinking
even though it's still morning.

At fifty my father had thirteen years left,
only ten of them any good.
I'm fifty-one and hoping my genetic
flaws are drawn more from my mother's side.

I look like her. More and more
in pictures my smile, the width of my face,
my dark, graying hair. But I have my father's
nose, and there's something that catches

in my throat, a sound I make
that's his. Is it better to go suddenly,
the way the paper says when
someone you know puts a gun against

her chest, or to spend those
last three years getting cut, getting thinner.
After the first cut, after he'd lost
maybe thirty pounds of muscle,

when we were riding somewhere
to some appointment,
through the park, I think it was,
through a tunnel of leaves,

I tried to pep him up, my sanguine,
saturnine father. He'd built his muscles
before, right? he could do it again.
What did I know about the body,

or about the weight
of absence, how it supplies a new
dark burden? I suggested meditation,
and he tried because he loved me,

but this was not my wry father's way.
Can you think away the cells?
Can you form repelling armies,
North vs. South as on that complicated

board game, Chancellorsville, that he studied
for hours one Christmas,
learning the rules.
The doctor told my mother

that, statistically, he had, maybe
three years. I was so young
that didn't seem so bad.
So much can happen in three years.

They can find a cure.
It can happen.
This morning, when I went outside
for wood, I found small paw prints

in the snow, leading up
to the cabin door.
I'd like to think it was a fox
or some other critter

scarce back in the suburbs.
But it was probably a feral cat,
cold and hungry, looking for the mice
I heard last night, rustling

the bag of peanuts I forgot to put away.
I got right up, went into the kitchen
and turned on the light: nothing,
so I put the peanuts away,

though later, lying in bed,
I began to worry about the mice.
Who'd take care of them,
if I didn't, if I denied them?

Is each mouse body a temple
as well? Is there some gray area
between the trap and
a plate of peanuts left,

like cookies for Santa,
as an offering to
the spirit of goodness?

The Reunion

Outside the citronella barrier
mosquitoes wait, invisible, held back
by flickering lines of flame along the rail,
an orange wall reaching up toward
branches hung low with magnolia cream,

blossoms bobbing in a light wind.
Someone slides the screen door open, stepping
out onto this platform, drink balanced,
to kiss a cheek, whisper a few words
into a cupped ear. Even out here

the music that rises from the basement,
funneling its way up stairs and out
of windows, loud incense to the ear,
keeps conversation brief, squeezed between
songs. The moon is only a part of itself,

curving in and out of clouds. She speaks
of a time, twenty years, the words
needing an extra breath, a gasp
to push them out, trailing off, harpoons
that dive deep. The surface becomes calm

again. We turn to talk of children, jobs,
vacations. Safe harbor in the present.
Dark shapes, the dancers below,
a kaleidoscope of friends, of phantoms,
woven between the railings, a parade

across the dark screen of French doors,
backlit by a light from some interior
room. What passes for wild abandon, close
as we get in these days when no one
is making love in the bushes, no one

is howling at the moon. Love turns to
affection, the surface of love, the risk
smoothed over. Days of careening off
each other like pool balls kissed
across the green table, gone. Love

moves with the songs, or with the memory.
Two o'clock, the ghosts of those who died
early seem to hang just beyond the rail,
their funerals like road signs
to the rest of us. The moon is only

a piece of itself tonight. You can stare
as long as you like, it won't burn.
A glider swings by itself on the porch.
The dancers drift off, to wake
groggy, late in the day.

Counting Hawks

They glide in slow circles above the fields
of dry September corn, dark eyes corkscrewing down
to catch the flicker of mouse or squirrel
out foraging this morning. We've watched them

for hours, my son and I, since crossing back
from the island to the mainland, where they appear
sometimes right overhead, balanced on the edge
of something we can't quite see. Jess's sleeping,

Abra's head in her lap, the rest of the big dog body
stretching across the back seat. Are they dreaming
of the wild ponies? Or the boy with his first hunting knife,
sawing away at a blade of dune grass, or the color

of the sky as the sun settled into the scrub pines
beyond our tent, the fire and the candles and the lanterns,
beyond the plum-gray clouds of mosquitoes blossoming up
from the fields of brush as the ocean wind changed direction.

Abra would chase the stick forever, returning
like a paddle boat, snorting, stick in her mouth,
her coat wet and shiny as the spade-tailed raven's.
She's more beautiful than any dog I've ever seen, you say.

She's your spirit animal, known to you in some past lifetime,
I think, remembering how you and I, years ago,
proposed to each other for all future lives. Now the hawks
are tapering off as towns thicken along the highway,

as we close in on the Bay Bridge, and our son,
reluctant to give up the game, begins to imagine hawks
in every sea gull, in all the patterns
of the randomly flying birds.

Blue Hydrangeas

Bunches of blue, bushels of blue. And if you say it over
and over, rolling it in your mouth, saying blue,
blue, it becomes a kite on a broken line,
disappearing in all that blue before circling back
to the memory flowers in your grandmother's yard,
where you see her stooping over, snipping off, carrying
by the armload to dry multicolored for winter vases.
Not roadside fields of gentians—flowers from
a different story, ones with a scent of wilderness
about them—but childhood or maybe even endless blue.
Not dark blue. Certainly not dark night of the blue soul,
forty days and forty nights blue. But shadow side
of the house blue. Good dog blue. Blue that can be counted,
kept track of by the bees, honeycomb blue. Bypassed
by hummingbirds who have eyes, beaks, for red only,
who are in too much of a hurry to pause at blue.
Tall drink of water, root to leaf to flower blue.
Not twilight or bat-wing, but nap-time blue. Not blue-jay,
but bluebird, happiness on your shoulder, sprinkler,
fan and open window blue. Not iceberg or porcelain,
but the kind that finds its way in through the ear,
going down the dark passage of nerve endings, playing pinball,
piling up enough points to win another free game or two,
tickling the little harp strings, the same small hairs
as a bathtub-boat breeze, as a wind that makes the laundry
flap with laughter on a line, all those white dresses
kicking up their heels, to perfection blued, blueing, blue.

Abracadabra

I'm trying to think like a dog, imagining her path,
her ridiculous haunches disappearing through the window
and out into the thunder and lightning, turning right,
stopping maybe to scratch at the neighbor's door until
the next rumble and crash—not music, not kettle drums
or the mountain gods bowling, but sheer anarchy, her body
a puppet on terror's string, misery's leash, no solace
of the big bed, of a warm human body to shake against,
a pillow to nose under, a hand to tell her no, stay.
And into the woods, past the old oak that fell in the storm,
where she'd find a clump of bushes to hide under

before the next boom drove her on, whip-crack of sound
and light, up the hill on the other side, and into
the neighborhood beyond, where I've searched over and over,
driving slowly all afternoon. And I'm calculating how far,
how fast a dog can run, beginning to think it's useless—
the way she'll close the gap between us if I pick up a stick,
hurl it into the air—and you and I have made our widening circles,
driving miles and miles away, seeing other big black dogs
with blue collars, others wearing their names on silver bones,
dogs who made me get out of the car to look closer,
though finally they weren't her, the one with the thumping,

mace of a tail: she's left bruises on your soft skin
with that tail; your arms are still scarred from her sharp milk teeth.
But she's older now, her chin whiskers turning gray,
and as we meet, regroup, and get ready to make our last trip out,
before darkness draws a curtain on our chances,
we talk about how she'll probably end up on someone's porch
who will call us in the morning. And even if not, even if we never
see her again, you say you're sure she won't be sad,
how the thing you love about her most is her buddha nature,
her way of moving through the temporary world,
she of the clicking toe nails, of the velvet body, the root beer eyes.

Hands

When I began to play the guitar again
my hands had forgotten. It isn't
like riding a bike—a thing learned
in a graveyard, on a quiet road, a
father running beside green hills,
blue ponds all around, hands,
his, steadying you, hands, yours, gripping
the handlebars with streamers, with wheels
turning, clacking with baseball cards
clothes-pinned against the spokes,
legs working to keep the bike going,
some unknown law taking over
as the father lets go, the body
centers itself and joins the legions of riders.
They, the hands, had forgotten patterns,
tics, popular things, and they put themselves
up in a fist beneath my chin, and they
folded themselves in my lap, and they
reached up one at a time to scratch the top
of my head, and I said, it's all right,
good dogs, let's begin again, let's circle
back and forward at the same time, you
left hand, don't worry about the pain
of arthritis, of tender finger tips,
someone is here today to help you find
your way around the old fretboard, and you,
right hand, faithful hand, make of yourself
a happy blur, a time-defying hummingbird,
a blue-veined street map. And they breathed
two sighs of relief. The right one took up
the pick; the left wrapped itself around
the old scarred neck; a light from
the basement ceiling found the red body,
the black knobs turned, electricity spoke,
the windows shivered with joy.

Mystery Schools

Mystery Schools

The Holy Order of MANS, Saint Petersburg, Florida, 1974

Dark morning, Brother John a shadow in the doorway saying
wake up, a rustling in the room, a movement of shadows
falling from bunk beds, feet slapping the floor, *where,*
why, I'm thinking, the way it will be years later, waking
in the chair next to the hospital bed, my father struggling with the sheet,
the summer moon full, *help me,* he says, a bad dream
we know, a worse one he wakes back into, blood in the urine,
bile on the lips, and I'm on my way across the courtyard,
the air wet and salted, dark shadows of tall palms,
gardenias spinning on their branches, following
a line of blue robes through the kitchen
where brothers and sisters cook in silence.

Father Dean

Kept from newspapers, books, televisions for a time,
from all that carries the mass mind, thoughts
gray and foggy, we wash each leaf on the rubber plants,
then I'm on my knees scrubbing cracks in tile
with a toothbrush, not at all sure how I got here,
knowing it has something to do with light. *What*
are you going to do about it, he asked, pipe clenched
in his teeth, fixing me with his farm-boy eyes.
You must leave mother and father, he said, *let the dead*
bury the dead.

Reverend Ruth

Holds up a card, hand painted, of the Empress,
her foot on the crescent moon, the world
green around her as she speaks of images deeper
than words. One Saturday afternoon I rode behind her,
peddling on the smooth straight streets
leading down to the Gulf. Hair let loose,
she wore cut-off jeans, and I thought
of how my friends and I felt we could share
love, how it ended with only, on my lips,
the taste of blood.

Street Patrol

In the evenings, when the lizards slide sideways from
the warm sidewalks, we go out two by two,
brother and sister in clerics, walking street patrol,
cutting across the fields of trash, out looking for trouble.
Walk counterclockwise around it, a man and woman
yelling in the street. *Whisper in the ear* of the man
who has another down, say, *can I help you,*
watch as puzzlement comes, anger goes. Visit the old men
in their rooms. Share your tobacco. Pass by the bird lady,
gulls and terns a shroud above her head,
her eyes the color of the water spouts, of the sharks
the old men catch, of the rays that flop on the red-stained floor—
one by one by breath transformed.

Lannice Gilly

Sits in the molding shed, trying to look busy
as less and less lumber sells.
He's gumming sardines and crackers, listening
to a country voice sing of silver thread
and golden needles. We spend our days counting wood
and sweeping dust into the road that curves right,
then twists to the train tracks,
rusting beneath catalpas, where the freight trains
rarely come. I see one: A vision
fashioned from boredom, pipe smoke, and rain.
No apparition of the white buffalo. No descent
into the cave of snakes.

Flowers

Spill out of the dumpster—
put in the basket with the ones I'll find
in someone's yard, or down in the fields
or beside the river stained bloody by cypress trees,
as you swim through sometimes gold or root beer brown,
where sea cows swim ballets, munch water lilies,
where I might walk one night on water.
Once I stood barefoot in a nest of fire ants—
went tubing down the river anyway—the priest healed me,
touched me on the crown, though my breath kept coming
hard, brothers and sisters floating in and out with the current,
the water black, tipped with fire.

Concentration Exercise

In the beginning is the orange, and in the end
is the orange, the one on my desk
that I come to each day. *Let nothing break
the concentration* as the mind goes
inside the skin, then down through the white sheath,
traveling deeper inside sections separating
like continents, down farther and into
one seed, that peels back, yielding layer after
layer of slippery skin until finally
nothing.

Elonia

Bring on the traveling Teacher, the one
with the white robe, the knotless cord,
who focuses light like a laser,
reaches in, parts the waters of my chest.
Let her take down her long dark hair,
let her ask *what did you see.* Let us swim
out in the Gulf, her white body
settling like a swan's, let the sun sink
like a flamingo in the evening sky,
the dolphins grin,
the waves break.

Burning Rain

It's a day to burn rain in the big pan,
a day to send it back on all the windows,
a day for rain inside and rain out. It's
a day to mourn the crash of the hard drive,
to be glad it isn't the stock market, that
words gone missing are not necessarily
such a tragedy, perhaps a potlatching in
a season of rain and reflected light on streets,
of a gray veil for the beginning of the day.
It's a day to burn shadows, to wash off
psychic effluvia, to scour the walls, to bag
the newspapers, to carry out empty bottles
in the blue plastic bucket and place them
by the side of the curb. It's a day to turn
on the Christmas tree and watch the angel
that does nothing but shine through its
corncob gauze at the top of the tree,
a day for a shutdown, an intermission,
to hold an old imaginary pipe and practice
blowing rings, a day to sit back and listen
to the sound of heat turning on and off.
It's a day not to think about putting
your affairs in order or storing nuts
for the winter or your mother's living will,
but a day to sit right where you are
while Vesuvius rains lava, while Hiroshima
and Nagasaki return to the elements, to molecular
threads. It's a day not to make decisions,

to hold them at bay, wolves outside
the campfire, red eyes blinking on and off,
a day to let yourself go down for the third time,
to breathe water, to be tumbled in the avalanche
until up and down and left and right lose
meaning. It's a day to conclude nothing
as much as possible, a day to empty
your pockets, to search for no patterns
in the bubbling of the fish tank, the
pinging of rain, a day to do no laundry,
a day to wipe out the other days, to spin
yourself dizzy. It's a day without sacrifices,
without suffering, a day before the beginning
or after the end, a Utopian day, a Marxist day,
a Freudian, Jungian, astrophysical, chaotic day.
A winter day, but not a tragically disconnected
kind of day, more Ovid than Homer, a day
that changes, but remains the same, not a
human kind of day, no marriages either, no plot
and complications, no climax, no struggling self
allowed in this day, just a succession of eye blinks,
of twitching facial muscles, of red blood beneath
the surface, of you padding through the house
in your slippers in a completely random fashion,
not practicing your circles like the winter pigeons
in yesterday's parking lot, not practicing your guitar,
not practicing placing dots on paper in random order,
but a day to have your egg in a small china egg cup,
to boil it in the merrily bubbling water, to order
the broom and pan, no, not order, request
the broom and pan sweep up the trail of crumbs,

to watch as they walk across water, turn bread
into fish, wine into more wine, a day to be
absolutely unsure of yourself, to breathe no fire,
eat no crackers, gain no weight, leave no parties,
bestow no blessings, build no bridges, burn no
sandcastles. Not a Newtonian day, but a particle
and wave day, a week at the beach and one
in the mountains day, a day not of Marley in chains,
but of Scrooge down off the cross, the rock rolled
away, a rock and roll day, not war and famine
and all the sins of time, endless rain, burning bush,
mountain top desert, but cat across the street
through the window, drops of rain falling
from the white porch pickets into a strip
of rainwater and leaves and reflections day.

Listening to a Friend Recite Shakespeare

At his fortieth birthday party, my friend was given
a Box of Death—filled with old Kerouac novels,
worn-out Chuck Taylors, and several bottles of mescal,
the kind with the worm in the bottom, the one they say
you shouldn't eat, but someone always does.
Also a Stratocaster guitar cake made by his wife.
At the same party, Jay, who I sometimes see
in the weight room, said he was just released
from the hospital—he took too many pain pills by mistake,
drank too many beers, and was found at the bottom
of the basement stairs. They wrote it up as attempted suicide.
When he woke in a room with one small glass eye

of a window and mattresses on the walls, he broke
the restraints and pounded on the door until
they came in, threw him down, and shot him up again.
Someone at the party wore snake-skin boots.
Someone else told of his dog, a German Shepherd,
that snapped a possum off a fence—pointing at
the white pickets that divide the backyard
from the woods, the afternoon leaves turning green
as bottle flies, nearly blue. One day the dog attacked,
dragged him to the ground, tore open his side.
He had to lie still until the dog, thinking he was dead,
left the room. He had no idea why. He loved the dog.

He's from the old neighborhood, and we talked
about the man who used to sell firecrackers
from the back of his convertible Caddy—Ladyfingers
we'd shoot from slingshots or put in coke bottles
and drop off the stone bridge, holding our breath until
like depth charges, they'd blow holes in the water.
He hates his job and would rather fish all the time.
Most of us cling to the weekends or evenings
when we can drink to forget the immediate past.
Sometimes when the weather's nice,
and I'm working out on the screen porch, I'll hear
my neighbors arguing—or really the man yelling things like,

Why are you fucking me in the fucking ass again?
The other morning this happened as the school bus
rolled by that parks at the bottom of our street—
the young driver hurrying to meet the woman
in the lipstick-red Mercedes. At the same moment,
the phone rang, and it was my wife telling me
about a woman who threw herself in front of a metro train.
Maybe she'll recover and be filled with grace. Or maybe
she'll look out through new eyes for a while and then
slowly begin to forget—the way the features on an old friend
begin to fade years after you've moved away, until you can't
remember a thing, until it's as if she never existed.

Exquisite Corpse

We'd mostly push wheelbarrows filled
with wet cement from the front
of a house to the rear, often on rickety,
jerry-rigged pathways made of boards.

There was a certain skill involved
in balancing the heavy loads, one
I never mastered, always wobbling
along, sometimes dumping a load

far from the swimming pool, drawing
disgusted looks from Frank, the foreman.
At the end of summer, I was laid off
from Coastal Pools, but found another job

working as a psychiatric aide. My job
was to mingle with the patients
and write my observations about
each patient's progress in a blue

spiral notebook kept by the nursing staff.
On Saturday there are no meetings,
so white paper rolls out into the morning,
twelve feet of tabula rasa, and we're

down on our knees playing
the exquisite corpse game. I draw
the head of a young, dreamy-eyed man,
a green traveling hat on his head,

blue sky and a sun behind him,
a few crooked birds. Gwen adds a torso,
a woman's curved body. Around
the conference room, people

play cards or watch cartoons, waiting
for time to pass, to start feeling better,
for someone to unlock the door
with a word. Bonnie draws a picture

of her lost son, her own face a large oval,
like a doll's, a madonna of confusion
whose thoughts tape-loop along,
always returning, never far from

the dead boy. But for now she's
coloring, choosing her crayons
carefully. People get better here,
or mostly they do, talking their way

through the stations of grief,
circling each day in groups,
swallowing potions, taking passes
to go for walks out in the world.

The Imaginary Ones

The picture window that darkens at night to a mirror,
where silhouette hawks turn back errant, mistaken birds,
reflects upon the Tom and Jerry parties your parents had
yearly, that we'd mill through, the living room ascending
to a peak of wooden beams, your uncle's geometric abstractions
hung, combined and recombined, the adults from another era,
you and I just passing through, their images reflected
in the glass, holding their drinks, getting cocktail happy.
And around the corner, where the picture window stretches
into the dining room where we dined one night before I left,
moved away, put on clerics, a collar and a cross on a blue ribbon,
changing before their eyes, before the candles and the silver
and the blackened, tree-wavering window, childhood falling
away, our friendship falling past the place carved by
easy conversation, the seamlessness of moving together
through close time, familiar space. The fireplace to the left
of the windows, behind the birch-white chairs, where my first love
and I lay beside it one winter day watching the snow fall before
or after we made love, before or after we went sledding or
grabbed our skates and went to the golf course pond
with our friends, school lost for a day, snow falling,
creating a silent gap, a parting of the waters of past and
future, she and I becoming what we were to parents,
what we were to each other, ideas of over spilling love.
Downstairs your father's records, his collection of musicals
in the shelves surrounding the T.V., where the ironing board
is set up, past the wall of New Yorker covers, and to the side
of the piano you learned on, wrote songs about Aunt Tillie
and blue pillows, where we'd get drunk when your parents
were away, when we could convince our friend
with the deep voice and hair that looked wiry and almost

gray to steel his courage, get into his role and stroll
nonchalantly into the Green Meadow's liquor store, pipe in hand,
the friend we loved to trick, carrying him draped over us
up the boulevard at dawn after a night spent drinking in the woods
behind the archery range, how cold it was even in spring,
we dunked his hand in water, made him piss in his pants,
he lost his shoe somewhere; I don't remember how he explained it.
Your bedroom to the other side of the New Yorker wall,
behind the door where your parents would tack up your
report card in shame, where you kept your match book collection
and your collection of band cards: Lawrence and the Arabians,
The Hangmen, the British Walkers—hundreds more, most
of which we'd seen together. A heavy curtain at the one
high window, where we'd go to talk and light incense, drink tea
and eat the brown bread you made when we felt like buddhas,
talking happily to each other about our other two selves, the ones
who didn't quite know what we knew, the imaginary ones.

Summer Time

Monday nothing, Tuesday nothing, Wednesday
a little more nothing the Fugs sang that summer as we
hung out in Tompkins Square Park, got spit at
by the Mothers of Invention, smoked banana peels,
hypnotized our friend into thinking the world
absurd—he rolled on the floor of that small apartment
laughing uncontrollably as we frantically counted
down to one, zero, and he stopped. Zero, nothing,
slug-a-bed, hammock drowsing mind going on vacation,
fleas and ticks in the grass, cancerous sun in the sky,
skin like warm air, air like warm skin, fans shoving

the thick air from one room to another, mind
freefalling through black holes and wormholes.
Summer time, maple syrup slow, days and nights
of television time, time to go back farther,
to read all the *Tarzan* books, and then the *Carter*
Man from Mars, walking to the book store
every few days, mosquitoes and June bugs
and fireflies and locusts whirring in the woods,
poison ivy and swimming pools and frozen Zero bars,
time to notice the girl across the street
is sprouting breasts, nipples that stand up

beneath her t-shirt, to give her little brother
whiskey that my parents keep beneath the sink,
to do a litany of stupid things, ones I'm capable
of doing even now, stupidity being something that comes
naturally, that, like riding a bike, you don't forget,
your father teaching you, riding wobbly along
the cemetery road, hands gripping the handlebars,
streamers streaming, baseball cards clacking in the spokes,
the ponds like mirages coming and going between
green hills, lazy turtles sunning on logs,
your father's grave waiting up near the road for

another summer, one of air conditioned bedrooms,
the cold, clear air a lie, the bees outside his window
a truth, the white, borrowed hospital bed a cipher,
a puzzle, him lying there as you bend over him,
watch him stop, the clock of the universe
going back to the repair shop, sand in the gears,
beach sand, summer sand he picked up swimming with
the dolphins off the coast of Nantucket or the Outer Banks
or in the Black Sea or down in the salt mines
where he took us one day, the shallow lake so salty
you can lie down without fear and float.

Happiness

I'm watering the new grass, positioning the sprinkler
so it will favor half of the yard with its fine, artificial rain.
I'm watching as the long lines splash up into the dogwood,

where a hummingbird darts from leaf to leaf, drinking or bathing,
seemingly delighted to find this small miracle on a hot June morning.
Whatever else is going on in the variegated, striated world,

the hummingbird and I, at this moment are happy. This won't last.
Sun-faced Buddha, moon-faced Buddha, the book I'm reading
is trying to tell me. But who doesn't prefer the sun-faced one,

and who doesn't get hopelessly attached to the idea, stuck
like Brer Rabbit in the Tar Baby of happiness? I have a friend
who seems most happy when she's bearing a grudge, when

she's miserable, all the wheels of her mind turning toward
this unprofitable idea. Is this what Keats means by bursting
joy's grape against his palate fine? I know this feeling,

this compulsion for revenge, this picking at the scab of a wound,
imagined or real, this rolling the rock of hurt up another hill.
Let me keep my hell, let me clutch on to it tight, at least it's better

than whatever else might come flooding in. But the leaves
on the dogwood laugh at this idea, and in the shadows numberless,
life and death struggles of small insects go on without mercy.

Larry Dodge

Larry Dodge is dead, died in a car crash in New Jersey
my mother's neighborhood paper tells her, and I'm thinking
of the time his father called us, *It's the last straw,* he said,
I'm kicking him out, his son crawling on the floor chasing
imaginary mice, another drug-induced vision. What I liked
about Larry was his goofy laugh and his long dirty fingernails
and the way he'd knock the ash off his cigarette and rub it
into his jeans. I liked his greasy dark hair, grown only as long
as his dad would allow, and his jean jacket and his love of Dylan
and the Stones—he named his first son Mick—and the way
he played the drums, cigarette stuck in his duck lips, and
the way he got me into trouble—no, I did that on my own—
with the younger sister of his girlfriend, for doing what she said
her stepfather did, who we'd visit during those hot summer days.
She didn't look as young as she was and I'd like to say I'm sorry
but I don't think either of us minded then and I hope she doesn't now.
My stepfather has a shotgun, she says, as we lie in her bed,
the room lit by only the light squeezing through the closed blinds.
But Larry's gone, no chance he'll be anywhere other than here
and there and a few other places, like back on that island
in the middle of the Potomac where we'd rowed the two canoes—
one painted like a giant trout—and pitched my parent's
old green army tent and toked ourselves into a weekend stupor.
It was my first time, and I smoked and smoked without feeling a thing
until I walked outside of the tent and into the dazzle of sunshine.

Tea Leaves

It was as if you'd gone away
on one of those business trips,
returning with maybe a steer's head string-tie
from Texas or a yo-yo or new top.
But this one goes on and on,
and to watch for you from some widow's peak
of the soul is useless, but even so,
that's what I do. Maybe its just fear or self-pity,
those emotions that nose up to the window
where living slows, your death
my soul wears like a hair-shirt
giving way to what was before
and what might be. *Father,*
a word that conjures up a great forest
of words, a word that like *death* or *love,*
seems almost insurmountable.
Was your life defined by sacrifice—
your father who preferred not to work,
who drifted from job to job,
the money you'd send him,
and then us, and how you found yourself
suddenly one day unhappy
in the job you had, negotiating
government contracts, how you once told me,
how you showed me by the way your
shoulders started to round, how hard it is
just to live inside one body every minute
of every day. But maybe these things
were choices, or a blending—
like soup, all ingredients forming
around one base, one stock, love
in your case, for my mother,
and the life that followed and the life
that came before focused on that point.
And there must have been a day, one moment
when you knew that your life would be happy,
that it was good, that your mother was wrong
when she read the leaves in the bottom
of your tea cup and turned away.

From a Hotel Window in Silver Spring

You died. This description could apply to many,
but it's you, Jay, I'm seeing from my hotel window,
moving slowly down the street, cane in hand. It's
a cold, rainy January day, and we're here in Silver
Spring, you and I—you, down there, making your way
across the street, the river Styx, no ferry man in
sight. It's been only a few weeks now, your body
found in the small room you called home, your back,
no doubt, acting up again, causing more and more pain,
each winter it seemed worse. I saw your mother
on the street, at least I thought it was, her ghost gray face
and hair, she who never believed you, who told you
to tough it out, straighten up. And you weren't always one
to be believed, not even your friends, who loved you,
could sort it out, the medications you carried, the way
you slurred your words, fell down. A few sea gulls
come and go, fly until they disappear, their wings
matching and then unweaving the sky. I was never
in your room, though I'd drop my son off to take the elevator
up, to come down again with a stack of magazines
you thought he might like, guitar players on all the covers.
He's got them still, his legacy, your generosity.
I see you waiting for the light to turn green, the color
of the money you do not have, or the willow trees
in our backyards in the ripe old summer days now gone.
Where did they go, each one an arrow shot into a target
at the archery range, or a can kicked until a mother's
twilight voice called us in, each summer a gathering of moths
against a screen door, flapping for a little more light,
for understanding what is beyond the memory moths,
that they only sense, know they need. The light turns,
and you hurry into the morning, a bus ride,
an odyssey of doctors, ahead, behind.

A Thousand and One Nights

The dog has just spit blood up on the floor
and she's lying on the rug, doesn't even
want to go outside to play ball, so let us
walk a while, Death, you and I. Don't be
impatient, I'll take your hand and you can walk
with me as we think on this a while, as we
stroll along a mental beach, watch her
churn the waves with her webbed paws,
hear the mermaids applaud from their side
of the ocean. What's that you say,
as you try, politely, to loosen my grip?
What is that you mumble, your words drowned
out by the ocean as it spills the dog out,
regroups, begins to listen for the call
to come in, begins to raise its pitch just
a bit, at the calling of the moon. She
whistles, the mother moon, out her back door,
she rings a bell, bangs a pan and the waves,
the dog, all the sandpipers and hermit crabs
ignore her for a moment, go back to what
it is they do. Not again, they all think,
not time to close up shop, we were only
beginning, we had just got our paws wet,
just dipped our snouts into the fragrant
grasses, only found that particular smell
just this moment, and who knows where it will
lead, who knows where it will lead.

The Sniper

The Sniper

1.

Though this didn't start with the sniper, who turned out
to be a man and a boy firing through a hole cut in the trunk
of a beat-up Caprice, it might as well have. It was after
a few weeks of this, of bushes rustling in the glittering dark
every time I'd leave the house, of the mysterious white panel truck
I'd never noticed before, now always parked just around the corner,
and of the bridges, especially the bridges, each one, even the one
over the Northwest Branch that I'd driven over how many thousand
times, that I began to dream, to wake and fall back asleep again,
and there I'd be on a bridge, staring down into a shallow river,
and there in the mud would be severed heads waving like cabbages
in the current, like jewels. I'd be driving across the Bay Bridge,
the one some terrorist and his wife had filmed, and suddenly
the bridge just stopped, all of the high wires, all of the gulls
and clouds and concrete and depth that I'd suddenly found unbearable—
the way my father could never climb a ladder, how he'd hold
the bottom as I goat-footed it up to the top to clean the leaves
out of the gutter, happy with the view. But in the dream, and more
and more in the un-dream, I felt unmoored, untethered, floating . . .
until suddenly it was over, the sniper part, the two led off in handcuffs,
though not the dreams. Did it have something to do with remembering
which breath, in or out, I'd been counting as I finally crossed over
into sleep, or the land above the clouds and through the windows,
or the plane as it made its way toward the Capitol building,
toward the Pentagon, toward my office in the city with a bull's-eye
painted on its back, where my wife works a few blocks away,
a gas mask tucked into the back of her desk.

2.

While standing at the urinal I thought of my childhood friend,
    Mike Parker,
who told us that fucking was when you put your weenie
    in a girl's fanny,
and the rest of us laughed hysterically, knowingly, since we were
    a few years older
and had seen the magazines stashed in the hollow tree by my friend's
    older brother
that described and depicted the more traditional definition,
    but my urinal vision
lasted only for a moment and then it was back to work, back to my
    office where I closed
the door, where at that time of the morning, I am rarely disturbed,
    not even by the sound
of people in the halls. I'm thinking now about lunch
    at Charlie Chang's,
how I got there first, sat down on the far side, with my back
    to the wall so that I
could watch for Diana, and as I sat by myself and started sipping tea,
    I thought
I'd practice being quiet, try following my breathing, and I must have
    looked suspicious
because the couple on my left began to lower their voices,
    though all around me
the sound of conversation and the scrape of silverware on plates
    happily continued.
It was only a few minutes later that I saw her through the windows,
    just before she
opened the door, her black hat pulled down against the wind,
    and we talked shop,
not sex, though cheeks were kissed, though she used the word
    vibrator twice,
and isn't sex always a current, though we notice it more as texture,
    as the hint of garlic

coming from somewhere in the restaurant that we don't feel compelled
        to track down.
We're mostly satisfied to go on with what appears to be
        our waking lives,
preferring the smoother rhythms, and maybe this is a function
        of being a little older,
more things having happened, not quite so willing, or needing
        experience as before,
say, when we were laughing at Mike and his face got red and
        he stomped away
having learned an important lesson, one which he would, no doubt,
        build upon
in the years that would spool rapidly by. Sometimes I hear my
        grandson's dolphin sounds
coming from downstairs, where he lives with his mother and father,
        and I'm saddened
by all that can go wrong, how I want to protect him, but I remember
        the film
that my wife and I saw last night, about the two Arab boys who
        couldn't find work—
they'd eventually die at the end of the movie, their boat-turned-bomb
        rammed into
a tanker—and one is telling the other that at Muslim school
        they serve lamb stew,
to which the other replies "I *like* lamb."

3.

Thursday's not quite the end of the week but close enough—
time to start seriously drinking, if we're those two people
we used to be, you and I in a booth at Town Hall, your knees
under the table brushing mine, the jukebox playing
you can't always get what you want, both of us knowing
this to be too true. You're engaged to Kevin, and I'm trying
not to feel what I'm feeling, I'm not even sure what it is
since we're at the beginning of what will be, the river
that will lead us here, just paddling around in the dim light
of the back room. You're wearing that white top
and those beat up jeans, holes in the knees, so your flesh
brushes as close to me as it will tonight, as we drink our beer,
pouring glass after glass from the pitcher. It seems harmless,
this current, we have no reason to believe it's deadly as love,
it isn't serious, these waves, these particles that travel
the watery air between us, your two dark eyes like searchlights,
like the lighthouse we'll look for sometime in the future,
driving with our son out to the tip of an island,
where we'll get out and find ourselves in a cloud of mosquitoes,
all hungry for our blood. We're hungry too, aren't we,
for each other. Our hunger feels good,
feels warm as the alcohol bathes the dark bar in a light
like you told me you'd look for, sometimes late at night
when the loneliness of your room was too much and you'd
have to leave, get out and drive through some neighborhood,
looking for the amber glow coming from a porch
or filtered through the curtains of an anonymous house—
one like we live in now, about ten miles away from that bar
along Route 1 that wasn't very popular with the other students,
more for serious drinkers, working stiffs, regulars, where
we could lose ourselves, where there were no claims on us
for a few hours, where we were nowhere, as if in some Dutch painting,
the booth the color of old velvet, of mahogany, of blood,
both of us listening to the jukebox oracle.

4.

Monday morning is the steep drop, the edge of the cliff, the time
    to practice
being the monk who finds himself hanging by one gnarled root
    between
the tiger above and the one below. It's the harbinger of difficulties
    to come—
you can almost see the phantom ship with its skeleton crew drifting
    through the mist.
And even though this morning comes a little later in winter and it's
    not as dark
as it could be when the alarm blasts, and the windows let in a few
    suggestions of light,
the sky like someone's blue shoulder scratched with red lines,
    all I can think
is how lovely it would be to crawl back under the three blankets, ·
    the top one
now covered with a shower curtain because the dog, who's only
    allowed up when the sky
gets light, who's happy now, is sporadically incontinent, and she's
    making the bed
crinkle with her heavy body as she settles down between us,
    the two lovers.

5.

There I am, on my knees scrubbing with a toothbrush,
and how many times have I thought of this, and it isn't even my story,
it's Reverend Ruth's, who has now gone back to being Vicky Beale,
living in Chicago, where she and her husband lived before they joined the Order.
But what relevance does the Order have for me now? It's like my father—
haven't I mourned enough? What would he have done these past 23 years?
Made my mother happier. I called her by mistake last night, told her
I'd meant to call my friend, and we spoke briefly. There was a gray note
to her voice as she let me go after only a few minutes, and I thought of her
alone in her small townhouse, with its windows looking out on the woods,
like those she remembers from childhood, as she circles back, the seasons
traveling in reverse. I gave her flowers, purple roses, for Valentine's Day,
thinking of my father and what he'd want, though he'd probably scoff,
his temperament not effusive. Somewhere Reverend Ruth is still scrubbing
a bathroom floor with a toothbrush, a job some master teacher gave her,
an Augean stables task she accomplished just before she came into one
of the initiations, I think it was the Self. I'm thinking of how, in the middle
of the two weeks that the sniper stalked Washington, I went online, looked her up,
then Master Tim, who I wrote, asking about the Self. A circular initiation,
he said, that keeps blossoming, and I think of Yeats's gyre, of the falcon
spinning away from the falconer, of a note and its harmonics, of someone
on her knees with a toothbrush, and someone holding his father's hand
as the last puff of breath rises into the room, and someone hiding
in a car trunk, shooting through a small hole cut in metal.

Astrodon johnstoni

Somewhere electronic church bells are telling the story
      of Sunday morning, and there's a breaking of the fast,
and people are either coming in or leaving, families dressed
      for ritual, bacon and eggs and pancakes, Sunday comics
opening at the sound of bells like the blue flowers
      that open for the sun each morning at my window.
There's the sound of a watch ticking. I think it's the one
      I lost that summer in the Nine Pond, that slid
off my wrist as I waved the net down under the green water.
      I think my grandfather brought it back this morning
as I was waking—found it in the drawer where he kept his ruby ring,
      his black-jack, and all the change he'd save and then
let waterfall down to this floor in the room where I'm
      almost sleeping, happy to have him back from where he's been,
where they've all been, grandparents, my father, the dinosaur—
      the one whose bones were found in the Laurel clay mine,
the one some legislator would have named our state dinosaur,
      star-toothed plant eater, stump-legged swamp wallower,
perhaps one that needed a second brain, one to guide the tail
      the way a fire engine needs an extra man in the back
as it takes the corners, bells clanging out of childhood.

The Black Swan

Someone's crushed it with a rock—
maybe no sadder than if it had happened
in the wild, pulled under by an alligator—
and I wonder what the boy was thinking
when he saw the sleeping swan, its long neck
smooth as a woman's, curled beneath
its wing. Perhaps it was only a joke—
the way someone will laugh and swerve
across the road to hit a possum, savoring
the irony of its fainting defense. Maybe
it's just the world going about its business—
like the squabbling sparrows I saw
on a branch outside the window, or the spider
that makes its home in a corner, up early
this morning, wrapping a lightning bug
that continues to weakly blink, or the croakers
my friends catch and throw back, named
for the word each knows meaning
I would grant you three wishes if I could.
Or it may have been beauty he had in mind—
the moment a mix of rock and feathers,
beauty born as the white swans rise
like thoughts in the night's dark zoo.

From a Buick Electra

The painted desert's painted blue tonight.
A screen of mountains at the eye's edge
modulates to sand, the sand to pavement
where the lines blur to a thin, pale stripe
at this speed. You've cracked the windows,
favoring the cool, desert breeze to the hum
of air conditioning, and as you sleep,
face against its own reflection, the wind
provides company, washing through the car,
replacing the radio we lost miles ago.
Sometimes a flash of neon, a truck stop
or gas station tugs at us to visit

its all-night world. But tank still full,
cruise control set, the Electra follows
the endless lines, while I simply steer
and try to stay awake, watching the wind
unweave your hair. Your legs fade,
stretching into the darkness beneath
the dashboard. We've no reason to be here,
traveling through peyote country, not far
from the graveyard of Cadillacs,
where they're buried nose down, fins
saluting—like an American Stonehenge.
Just now, Love, before the synapses could

fire, a dark moon came spinning out, cast off
like a truck driver's cigarette,
took a bounce, arced across the windshield
close enough to catch the scent of rubber,
to see the torn thread for a long instant
before it landed, on a whim, in the road
to vanish. If you woke, you would see the sky
beginning to gray, the forked shapes
of cactuses reaching up out of sleep,
brushing off clouds of wrens, and a trickle
of red in the mirror—taillights reflected,
or the morning spilling across wild land.

Twelve-tone

This morning between your legs the world
is wet; between the layers of blankets
and the mattress and two floors up
from the hard cold ground, you're moving back
and forth, and though our son sleeps
in the next room you're singing softly,
the only sound this could be, a note
or an octave or a fifth, fourth, a ninth,
an harmonious tone or a strange, nearly
disconnected twelve-tone banging
of a garbage can lid or the caw of a crow,
or a snap of a mouse's broken back,
or the sound of a man fallen into the water
who's just gone up on deck to smoke a cigarette
late at night, the door he'd forgotten
to close swinging open.

Atlantis

How is it she comes back, resurrected,
always rising like the corn, her body like yours
spread across the motel bed, the ocean still outside,
the rain mapping the sand, the doorway open,
pelicans and gulls drawn in gray and blue. The waves
whisper outside these doors, where desire undresses
each one slowly, first curling as far and as slow
as the eye can see, then building power until the horizon
comes closer, is there at your feet, where you grow
out of the ground, rooted a moment more, before you go
with her and everything tastes of salt and honeysuckle,
the one drop from each bitten, cream-brown flower.
Her legs are here and then there, the nape of the neck,
the shoulders, the grains of sand, clear and white
as sugar that roughs the skin, that bruises the soft inside
of a thigh, the goddess reclining like the history
of the world. And then the instant it takes to see flowers
on the table, Queen Anne's Lace and Black Eyed Susans,
a thousand eyes bring you into the room,
where the mist curls as she looks up, her hands behind her,
over her head now and beneath a pillow as if grasping
through the clouds for something just beyond
the headboard and through the wall in the next room,
where mermaids become human with desire, and Atlantis
lies buried. You'll soon see if the mist rolls off,
if the announcer gets it right, the one whose blurred voice
you hear somewhere between the bands of static
the waves make, the sheets make, she makes as she moves,
rolling between planes, fingernails long and red as poppies,
as your bodies rise from the waves of sheets
like the backs of dolphins beyond the black rocks,
or the blink of the lighthouse down the coast,
a warning rising up against the sky for ships
to come no farther, that beyond that point,
they must not go.

Gettysburg

Two speckled horses graze in the field
we look across, where musket balls,
once thick as twilight, kissed in air, fused
and fell. There must be more, our son says,
as he kicks the ground, wishing to raise the dead.
Some rise slowly year by year on the roots of trees;
some travel farther down into the underworld.
I think of Stonewall Jackson, who might have turned
the war, the world, slain by his own men,
mistaken at dusk, ghost-gray darkened to blue:
the irony of the gods of war, the winds
changing with a puff from great, immaterial cheeks—
like Patroklos, caught with the wrong shield.
I would leave you if you were untrue. I would
kill you if you were untrue is the song
that seems to float over mountains and fields.
And he took her down to the river. . . .

Morning Song

1.

Night somewhere lost in the blue buzz,
in her scent of sleep, her arms curled, her name—
the one you know from the land of dreams,
a mirror to the faint light through the windows,
earthly stars, or remembrance of stars, light that falls
the way you do now as you reach out to touch—
not to wake—this skin like a river, with its eddies
and currents, the way it moves above the continent
of bones. The light leaves her as she shifts
and her hair falls into the worlds of dust
that surround you, instants of continuance
through separation, the way your hand
follows its thought beyond the dark house,
through planets of hours to come.

2.

Waking, I can't shake the feel of death's lips,
of air that lies still and won't move on,
piss yellow, pill-bottle green, outside and all through
the screen, the small square holes slicing it into
a thousand pieces. The angel knows when
each one's time has come, my time, her lips
just brush me now, say, wait, go back to sleep,
not yet, no rustle in the dry leaves, no sound
of difference, wait, go fix yourself some coffee,
watch out for traffic, turn on the radio.
There are voices in the air, dark holes of spirits,
husks and shells of cities, empires.

3.

I wish she'd shout *there it is*, I wish we'd say *always*
to each other and dance madly around a maypole,
our carnival of flesh falling away, our corpse dance
over the burning coals, right through the iron lady,
her dark doors shutting, both of us jolly,
all of us happy as oysters come to the party.
Buy me a beer, won't you, tell me what it is
that's rumbling around, lend me an ear,
the tip of a tongue, friend, with your silky arm,
your long neck. Let's take my red car
to those blue highways that spread out like
these veins. We can breathe our life into smoke,
we can make it rise up to stars, into ohs,
click your jaw like this.

4.

Metal-tongued birds—company this morning—
clamor at the ancient ball of fire. I remember
this window. You and I owned it for our brief
stay here, when we were in-between, our elbows
on the ledge, our faces against the screen,
honeysuckle rubbing us raw. If you loved me.
If I loved you. There they go, the birds' brass band,
wondering again. Outside, a worker is on the street.
A gray car passes. If your body passed ten thousand
times through these rooms. If you wore nothing
but garlands of lilies and roses. Both or either,
the way a hand will softly stroke a cheek, or one
pain will curve, blend into another greater, the worse
stretching beyond, as when one domino clacks
into another and then another until a great line falls
all through the house.

Stigmata

I'm imagining myself up on one of the crosses, let's say
the left one, looking downhill, and you're there beside me,
but you're nailed so you'll go quicker than I—and the other
guy, who will slowly sink, choking on our own rib cages.
And it's going to rain, it's going to storm, the sky's darkening
but the soldiers take no notice; they're used to all of this,
they're hardened to the elements, and the times are savage.
You can't speak or I can't hear you. We all have our jobs
to do, our rules to follow—don't eat meat on Friday,
don't work on Sunday, maybe spend ten years kneeling
in prayer, or learn to give it all up by sitting
beneath a Bow tree in the lotus position. Now you're
looking up—although maybe this is not so; maybe
you're turning to look over at me, sorry because you know
I'll be hanging here longer, that there's nothing you can do
about it—or maybe you're beyond sorry, there under
your thorn crown, your one life leaving quickly now. Maybe
there are angels, whatever they might be, hovering around you,
waiting for the right moment to do their job, to lift your body
up, transforming it—will it be made of real light, is that real
blood I see, are those real tears that roll down the cheeks
of plaster saints all over the world, real wounds on the hands
and feet of the priest in Lake Ridge, who has no idea why but
doesn't doubt anymore, who says yes, it is real pain, that
sometimes he can't sleep, that it wakes him up at night.

A Hunger Artist

On the path through the woods: a photograph, polaroid nearly in the water, as if it fell from someone's pocket, of a young girl, maybe sixteen, naked, lying on a bed, her hands over her breasts, her right leg crossed over her left leg, her figure full, her olive skin smooth, her eyes looking away from the camera as if she didn't really want this picture taken, as if this kind of guilt went beyond lying there, maybe on her parents' bed, in the late morning or early afternoon—you can't tell from the picture, only the figure on the sheets, a dark wood headboard behind her, blank white walls, and a nightstand with a white telephone that seems about to ring. You don't see all of this immediately. You pick up the photo and put it quickly in your pocket, wondering as you do if this is a trick, like the wallet on a string your friends dangle across a sidewalk every April Fool's Day, snatching it away from greedy hands, the group of them hanging from their office window and braying. But the woods are empty; you can easily see through the winter trees, the leafless branches, and the dog you walk is not often surprised, her sense of danger more primitive, or momentary, than yours. You think you will burn it, or tear it up, but you feel an undertow, thinking of her crossed legs in your pocket. Later, sitting in your car with the engine running, you'll think about the sky above the ice skating rink where your son goes round and round, the evergreens that sweep the air, and then about Kafka's story, wondering about how much is enough, the artist's death, ribs poking up through the straw, and the second ending, the panther in the cage, the raw meat.

The Natural World

Did you know that the mosquito
pisses on you before flying away,
heavy with your blood, and that
in a certain mood, you might take
this as an emblem for things as
they are, the natural world
being itself, and that you scratch
until the other nerve receptor,
the one for pain, takes over,
your fingernails, your skin, the miles
of instantaneity that you call you
engaged in its primary mode,
a scratching sharpened past annoyance,
pain relieving you of any other
possibility, until you become a mole
swimming through dirt, your eyes
nearly useless, or a mole-man living
beneath the streets of a city,
or a black hole unto yourself,
dense with matter, with lack of
light, disturbed by the slightest
itch of another theory, unable
to brush her away and forget.

Cruelties

I'm not thinking about Jeffrey Dahmer,
really a nice man, his shrink said, who
might have ended better if his experiments,
his home-made lobotomies, had yielded
a sex slave, not just corpse after corpse.

It's those earlier ones, the fish my friends once
caught, stuffed with a cherry bomb and threw back,
or the young retarded girl they'd talk about,
how she'd let them spread her legs, put a lit
cigarette in her pussy, so the pussy

looked like it was smoking.
I probably didn't believe this story, but
snickered along with them, the two brothers
who grew into men before we lost touch.
But I know I shot birds for no other reason

than to see them die, falling from their branches,
and squirrels—proud to take aim, freeze one
in mid-leap, bring it down, broken. I have
friends who hunt still, but I don't mean to pass
judgment—many years past being vegetarian,

living inside a body that has dealt out pain.
When I run my tongue over my teeth it stops
on those sharp ones. When I look at myself
naked in the mirror I know there's not much
I couldn't be made, twisted, called upon to do.

Bored

Tonight I'm lying on the railroad tracks,
the Virginia stars fixed uncertainly
in the black sky, my buddies beside me,
the three of us, who tomorrow the engineer
will say looked like cardboard boxes,
and we're almost sure that the train
will pass over us—as why wouldn't it?
And if it doesn't I guess it won't matter.
What else is there to do, the summer so deep
and green? Some might wake up tomorrow
and think us foolish to lie down between
the tracks, to hold our breath, to sink
as far as we can into the still warm gravel,
wishing ourselves below the rails.
And the whiskey makes me feel the way
I did when my father used to pick us up
and spin us dizzy, whirling us around and
around like two hands on a roaring clock.

A Different Law

My father never wept, or I never saw him,
not through the long months that the cancer
chipped away, finally cut him down to marble,
to a white, blue-veined man lying in bed,
glowing with light. Not in all the days
that contained, continued into nights, when he
walked through the rooms of our house as if
he couldn't decide, couldn't make up his mind
about something, settling for a few moments
in a living room chair, thinking better of it,
running the water for a bath. The house dimmed
to a murmur, a low current of sleeping bodies,
through the hours given over to owls, moths,
hours that for a time nearly cease being
hours, bending like light around the far corners,
looking for a different law. I close my eyes
and see him lying on his back in the ocean,
face and feet pointing up to blue nothing,
and I wonder about the body's affinity for salt,
how it lies there in the displacement,
in the womb, dreaming of the great land bridge,
and before, when the continents were one,
before marshland turned to Sahara. And now
bones of the first giants awaken, protrude
five hundred miles from any road, and Titans
become whales, then men, then one man,
there in the cool water, unable to sleep.

The Kiss

Wait. The chapel angel will be with you,
he said, for the next three days, just
kneel and pray and meditate. Cleansing
is what he calls it, like a cold that burns
away the dross, like the sun that burns
away the morning mist. Wait. But the stream
does not clear. The mad monkey runs
through the house. The great whale swims
too deep. A light comes up from the chest
and then dims again. The chapel angel
whispers, but its holy breath sounds
only like air conditioning. Sleep.
You are not this, not that. Lines intersect
like telephone wires that grid the city,
like a spider web built to catch a fly.
Your sad father walks from his end
of the glass hallway. It's no one's fault
your mother says, as she prepares you
for the white hospital gown and the slippers,
for the shoulders beginning to hunch.
Happiness, your father's told you,
is the key, and you wonder just how
this can be found. He is less strong,
you think, his muscles, he must not be
doing his isometrics here, he must not be . . .
what can he be doing to fill the days,
is he reading *Moby Dick* again, is he
working on his pottery, will they let you
bring your guitar here next time so
the two of you can sing together? You
can do anything you want to do, born

at mid-century, born on the day
the god of the well looks up and begins
to climb, as the earth, the hemisphere
stirs, hears the trumpet call, as
the great cave bear feels wakening hunger.
Failure, he says, is a gift, the hanged
man, the body turned upside down, the kiss
of Judas without which there is no next act,
it's Genghis Khan dragging the quickening
future with him, the murderer who meets Buddha
on the road, Saul knocked from the horse,
spirit and flesh fused as hammer and nail,
father and son at the center of the cross.

Acknowledgments

Grateful acknowledgment is made to the following publications
in which these poems first appeared:

Boulevard: "Stigmata" and "Stories"

Green Mountains Review: "Gettysburg" and "A Thousand and
One Nights"

Hayden's Ferry Review: "The Natural World"

Indiana Review: "From a Buick Electra"

The Literary Review: "Counting Hawks," "A Different Law," and
"Morning Song"

Mid-American Review: "The Black Swan"

The Midwest Quarterly: "Burning Rain"

The Nebraska Review: "Blue Hydrangeas" and "Without"

Poet Lore: "Exquisite Corpse"

Poetry East: "Abracadabra" and "Hands"

Poetry Northwest: "Atlantis," "Bored," "The Kiss," and "Hunger Artist"

Salmagundi: "Cruelties" and "Astrodon johnstoni"

The Sewanee Review: "Behind the Walls," "Connections," and
"The Butter Knife"

Sonora Review: "Mud Angel" and "Kozlow"

The Sycamore Review: "From the Mesozoic" and "In a Cabin
in the Woods"

WordWrights: "Twelve-tone"

I would like to express my deepest gratitude to Victoria Chang, Henri
Cole, Michael Collier, Sarah Ely, Edward Hirsh, David McAleavey, Faye
Moskowitz, Stanley Plumly, Carly Sachs, Jane Shore, and the members
of Washington Writers' Publishing House for their advice, encourage-
ment and friendship. And for their love and support, I wish to thank
my family—Doug, Lucie, Sam, Ann Marie, and Jackson.

I would also like to thank The Academy of American Poets,
The Association of Writers & Writing Programs, Bread Loaf Writers'
Conference, and Maryland State Arts Council for their generous
support.